Fifty Years of
Canadian Landscape Painting

Fifty Years of
Canadian Landscape Painting

A Selection

April 3–May 2, 1987

Karen Wilkin, Curator
William M. Chambers III, Co-curator

GRACE BORGENICHT GALLERY
724 Fifth Avenue, New York 10019   212/247-2111

The history of Canadian art is largely the history of landscape painting. That is not surprising in a vast country—second in size only to the U.S.S.R.—with a small population that even today is concentrated in a narrow band stretching from ocean to ocean. Canada is not only sparsely populated, but enormous sections of the country have never been inhabited; it is the antitheses of the Old World countryside, shaped by man's presence over thousands of years. The proximity of so much virgin territory where man is an intruder or, at best, merely an observer, has affected the national consciousness. Modern Canadians, for all their sophisticated cities, their century old farms and their high tech industries, still like to think of themselves as having a special relationship to untouched nature. The lakeside or island cottage, proudly devoid of electricity or indoor plumbing, is a status symbol. Summer camps turn urban children into tireless canoeists and adaptable woodsmen. Professionals, unwillingly tied to city residences, spend autumn weekends waiting in damp duck blinds for a flock to settle. (I know a Toronto painter who hunts bear, in season, with a bow and arrow.) This fascination with the real out of doors is paralleled by a continuing fascination with the *appearance* of the natural world, as reflected in Canada's art.

At first, Canadian landscape painting was bound up with a young country's growing sense of itself as a nation. The widely disparate provinces and territories that joined in confederation in 1867 were finally linked coast to coast by railway service in 1886. Waves of immigrants followed the new railroad across the continent, in a kind of Industrial Age version of the wagon trains that settled the American west, earlier in the century. Artists, too, crossed the country, at the invitation of the railroad companies, to record the scenic highlights of the route. They were usually members of the Royal Canadian Academy, mostly English-trained, frequently English (or European) born. They documented

the beauties of the new nation in a traditional, conservative manner. The Canadian Rockies or the Swiss Alps—it didn't matter. There were artists who concentrated on more intimate subject matter in more personal ways, but the painters of waterfalls and gorges, heroic mountains and limitless prairies, were greatly admired.

By the turn of the century, the new nation was producing native born artists but the most serious and ambitious went abroad to study. The most adventurous—many from French Canada—went not to England nor to the Düsseldorf Academy, which was highly regarded by their 19th century forbears, but to more forward looking institutions in Paris. They learned Impessionist techniques and attitudes, and when they returned home, they painted Quebec's Eastern Townships as though they were the banks of the Seine. Fields of snow became substitutes for fields of poppies. What water was to the French Impressionists—a light-reflecting, light-diffusing surface—ice and snow were to the Canadians.

The parallel evolution of a Canadian school of painting and a Canadian sense of identity echoes similar developments, somewhat earlier, in the United States. Through much of the 19th century in both countries, landscape painting catered to a combination of curiosity and nascent national pride. With the invention of photography, a new medium able to record natural phenomena in meticulous detail, was available to supplement the function of landscape artists. With the advent of modernism, painters claimed new tasks for themselves. What is remarkable is the vigorous persistence of a tradition of landscape painting in Canada. It has been transformed by modernist notions, or perhaps it would be more accurate to say that is has simply absorbed modernism. In marked contrast to the United States, the history of 20th century art in Canada is as much a history of landscape painting as that of the 19th century.

With few exceptions, traditional ideals still obtained among Canadian artists of the first part of our century. Modernism had virtually no advocates north of the 49th parallel. (There was no equivalent of the International Exhibition of Modern Art—the 1913 Armory Show—that introduced Americans to the most challenging art of the period.) Affluent Canadians collected, for the most part, the kind of academic, dark brown pictures that European modernists had reacted against. But a number of young painters in Toronto were beginning to think about art in new ways. In 1913, two of these young men, Lawren Harris (1885-1970) and J. E. H. MacDonald (1873-1932), travelled not to the Armory Show, but to Buffalo, to an exhibition of contemporary Scandinavian painting at the Albright Art Gallery. The show included works by three generations of artists, including many landscape painters who had absorbed new ideas and methods in the major European centers and then applied what they had learned, filtered through a kind of northern mysticism, to their own inhos-

pitable landscape. It seems absurd to speak of an epiphany in Buffalo, but MacDonald and Harris were enormously excited by the snow-filled images of the Scandinavian wilderness. The pictures that interested them most were not the most radical, but rather straightforward renderings of an oddly familiar landscape, painted in a broad, post-Impressionist manner. Yet they were not simply records of appearance; they suggested the insignificance of man in the face of omnipotent nature. MacDonald and Harris felt they could paint Canada in a similar way. They had already begun to explore similar subject matter; the Scandinavian

pictures provided both confirmation of their direction and encouragement toward a more adventurous approach to their motifs. To a great extent, the ideas Harris and MacDonald carried away from the Buffalo exhibition and handed on to their friends and colleagues in Toronto helped to form Canada's first clearly defined national movement in painting, that of Tom Thomson and the Group of Seven.

Toronto's art community was small and close knit at the time. Many of Harris and MacDonald's friends, Tom Thomson (1877-1917), Franklin Carmichael (1890-1945), Frank Johnston (1888-1949), Arthur Lismer (1885-1969) and Frederick Varley (1881-1969), were designers at the commercial art firm, Rapid Grip, where MacDonald worked. They lunched at the Arts and Letters Club and exhibited together in the Canadian Art Club's seasonal shows. A. Y. Jackson (1882-1974), a Montrealer, recently returned from a year and a half in Europe, soon became part of the circle, sharing a studio with Thomson. The young men went on sketching trips together, to the lake dotted country north of Toronto. Thomson was probably the best woodsman, respected by locals as a good fisherman and a skillful paddler who knew the north country intimately. Jackson was the most sophisticated painter, friendly with some of Montreal's most accomplished artists and fresh from his studies in Paris, where he had learned Impressionist *plein air* methods. Jackson and his friends painted on the spot, producing small, intense oil sketches on panels that fitted into their paint boxes. They painted the 19th century sublime, in purely 20th century terms: images of isolation and rigor, evocative of the power of nature and of man's ability to both survive in the indifferent wilderness and be transfigured by it. The group's declared intention was to express Canada's essence in ways that had nothing to do with European prototypes. Yet the simplicity, intensity and directness of their vivid sketches and the canvases they developed from them owe a great deal to Post-Impressionism. Their clear palette owes as much to Jackson's Impressionist training as it does to the light and air of northern Ontario. Their sinuous drawing and flattened shapes owe something to the Art Nouveau advertising art produced by Rapid Grip. But whatever their derivation, the group's pictures were radically unlike the romanticized academic landscapes so familiar to Canadian audiences of the time.

Carmichael, Harris, Jackson, Johnston, Lismer, MacDonald and Varley first exhibited together in 1920: the debut of the Group of Seven. (Thomson had died in an accident in 1917.) Their brilliantly colored paintings startled Toronto viewers and were greeted with the outrage and derision that the first Fauvist exhibitions had provoked in Paris. The first reviews were so bad that Johnston permanently disassociated himself from the Group; A. J. Casson (1898-) took his place. Very soon after the initial showing, however, the iconic power of the Group's images and the accuracy of their vision of the Canadian wilderness won them increasing attention. By the mid-1920s, their paintings had come to dominate Canadian notions of what art should be. Their autumn foliage, their wind-sculpted trees, their jagged rocks and storm-whipped water were images that corresponded to many Canadians' idea of their relationship to nature; they were quickly accepted as true visions of the quintessential Canada. In 1931, the Group more or less disbanded, but it continued to exist in an altered form in the association of like-minded painters who had been invited to exhibit with the Group during its "official" days. Jackson's old friend, Albert Robinson (1881-1956), showed with them as guest, while Edwin Holgate (1892-1977)—among many others—was a full-fledged member. Throughout the 1930s and much of the 1940s, the ideology of the Group and the look of its pictures set a standard for Canadian artists.

Things in Toronto changed very little for young painters in the 1930s. The once radical Group was now the establishment; a Depression economy kept even the most serious

artists from studying abroad, but in most respects, life for an aspiring painter was very much the same as it had been in the 'teens and the '20s. Young artists still worked in commercial art studios. Jack Bush (1909-1977), for example, was at Rapid Grip. Young Toronto painters still attended art classes and sketch groups, after work. They sent their pictures to Society and Academy shows, and joined the Arts and Letters Club. Bush and his friends, Charles Comfort (1900-) and Carl Schaefer (1903-), studied watercolor at night. One of their colleagues, later Bush's partner in a successful advertising art firm, described what it was like to be an ambitious Toronto painter at the time: "We were a little put off because it looked as if to be a good painter, you had to handle a canoe." Bush and his friends described themselves as "city lads." Instead of the Algoma wilderness or Algonquin Park, they painted their city neighborhoods, or remote parts of Toronto at the end of the streetcar line; sometimes they painted at the comfortable settled lakes where they vacationed with their families. "We belonged to what was known as the 'Cold Buns School'—we sat on stony hillsides...This has been a tradition in this country—to sit on stony hillsides and paint whatever you see." Comfort soon developed a personal realist style and a particular facility with watercolor, but Bush struggled to make his pictures turn out as much like the Group of Seven's as possible. He never succeeded. "They always came out Bushes," he complained, and recalled how worried that used to make him. It took years for him to realize that his unlikeness to the Group, his remarkable sense of color and his ability to invent eccentric shapes were strengths. Bush later abandoned recognizeable imagery and became internationally known as a deeply original abstract painter, but his early work is a graphic record of his effort to meet accepted expectations and, at the same time, to declare himself. Bush's earliest landscapes are at once hopeful responses to the example of the Group of Seven and reactions against it. Through the 1930s and '40s, we can chart the emergence of his new and more individual approach to familiar subject matter. At some level we are still aware of the overwhelming authority of the Group, but in these early pictures, Bush already uses shapes, colors and configurations that prefigure the mature abstract paintings that established his reputation.

The Group of Seven may have been Canada's officially recognized exponents of modernism, but there were important and gifted Canadian painters who developed innovative approaches to the landscape, quite independent of the

Group's example. Emily Carr (1871-1945) and David Milne (1882-1953), two of Canada's finest painters, invented personal and expressive ways of interpreting their surroundings. Apart from brief, relatively early exposure to mainstream vanguard art, both Carr and Milne worked in virtual isolation, unrecognized until the end of their lives. Their reputations have caught up with their abilities only in the past twenty-five years.

Carr, born in Victoria, British Columbia, studied art in San Francisco and later in England. A determined spinster, she went to Paris in 1910 and through her studies attached herself to the outer fringes of the Fauvist circle. She exhibited two lively Fauvist pictures in the 1911 *Salon d'automne*, along with Matisse and other advanced artists—and, it must be admitted, hundreds of others, as well. Poor health forced her to return to Victoria, where she struggled to support herself and to continue to paint. She applied the lessons of Fauvism to her native landscape, inventing rhythmic pictorial equivalents for the magnificent forests of the west coast; the rich, but vanishing culture of the west coast Indians also attracted her deeply. Despite their differences from Group of Seven precedents, Carr's paintings most often deal with untouched, awe-inspiring nature in the raw, so it is not surprising that she was befriended, towards the end of her life, by Lawren Harris, who admired both the audacity and the mystical, symbolic qualities of her pictures. Helped by this connection, Carr began to exhibit with some success across Canada. Unfortunately, she died soon after beginning to enjoy some degree of recognition.

Milne, born in Ontario, went to New York in 1904, to study at the Art Students' League, supporting himself as a commercial artist. He was exposed early to modernist notions, possibly through his associations with Maurice Prendergast. By 1913, Milne was painting highly simplified, brightly colored, light filled paintings of city scenes. He exhibited some of these in the juried American section of the Armory Show. These early years of study and the concentrated dose of modernism the Armory Show provided gave Milne a foundation for his art that lasted for the rest of his life. He soon left New York, retreating gradually northward, first to upstate New York and finally to a rural town outside Toronto, but he continued to paint in ways derived from his early experience of advanced French art. Like Carr, Milne invented a wholly personal kind of landscape painting, translating the essential shapes of trees, buildings, hills and ponds into spare drawing and economical color patches. Large areas of black and white isolate and intensify detached lines and color shapes and, at the same time, become equivalents for light. Milne's are among the most daring pictures painted in Canada at the time. Not only are they unusual for their formal innovation, but they present us with a new attitude toward nature. Milne's landscapes are benign, not awesome; they are often pastoral, tamed, changed by man. Flowers grow in gardens or are even gathered in vases. Milne's woods are second-growth, not virgin forests.

The pattern of Milne and Carr's development—a lifetime of ambitious painting sustained by relatively short, but significant encounters with major art—is repeated in the careers of two notable western Canadian painters. Maxwell Bates (1906-1981) and W. L. Stevenson (1905-1966) spent most of their lives in Calgary, Alberta, hardly a center of advanced painting in the first half of this century. Local standards were set principally by English artists who taught at the Provincial Institute of Technology and Art. The Group of Seven's influence had penetrated as well, through A. Y. Jackson's visits to the Alberta branch of his family and his later involvement with the Banff School of Fine Arts and through westerners who studied with Group members in eastern Canada. Stevenson and Bates met first at the Calgary Art Club's drawing classes and later became fellow students at the local art college. Together, they began to explore French modernism. With Bates providing the lead, they studied Roger Fry and Clive Bell's writings and magazines such as *The Studio*. Even though they knew advanced European painting only from reproductions, they were electrified by the possibilities they sensed in the work and strove to assimilate these new ideas into their own painting. In 1926 the pair was permanently barred from exhibiting with the Calgary Art Club because of their unorthodox tendencies. A year later, their enthusiasm was vindicated and strengthened when they travelled to the Art Institute of Chicago to see a special exhibition of Impressionism and Post-Impressionism. For three weeks they studied pictures by Monet, Seurat, Cézanne and Van Gogh. For Stevenson, this was the grounding for the entire development of his painting. (His next serious art viewing trip, to Toronto and New York, was in the late '50s). Bates was similarly fascinated, but the experience was tempered by his later studies of painting and architecture in England—where he lived for many years—and by two years at the Brooklyn Museum School. The economical expressionist styles developed by Bates and Stevenson are evidence of their uniqueness among Alberta artists of their generation, both for the variety of their influences and the progressiveness of their taste.

French Canada escaped much of the dominance of the Group of Seven, despite the powerful influence exerted by Arthur Lismer, from his position at a school affiliated with the Musée des Beaux-arts. A more important counter-influence was provided by John Lyman (1886-1967), when he returned to Montreal in 1931. He had lived abroad, mostly in France, for almost twenty years. Lyman remained peripatetic; he later spent a great deal of time painting in the Caribbean. Lyman had studied with Matisse and had been loosely associated with the French avant garde during his years of self-imposed exile. His paintings were distinguished by firm structure, solid drawing and intense (but not outrageous) color. Compared to Fauvist pictures Lyman's canvases seem robust but subdued, but Montrealers responded to his first exhibitions with horror. Ironically, Lyman became the generating force that radicalized Montreal artists, indirectly creating Canada's first group of wholly abstract painters, *Les Automatistes*. Lyman founded what became known as the Contemporary Art Society, an informal artists' association that provided members with news of the latest avant garde developments, with magazines and books that reproduced work never seen in Montreal, with opportunities to exchange ideas, and—most important—with occasions to exhibit. The Society helped to organize Monteal's version of the Armory Show, in 1939, a haphazard assortment of European art in Montreal collections, ambitiously titled "Art in Our Day". Lyman recruited promising young painters to the Society,

and in 1932, on the strength of a show of watercolors at the Arts Club in Montreal, he invited a young man called Goodridge Roberts (1904-1974) to join. Lyman said that Roberts' pictures made him excited about the work of a Canadian for the first time since his return.

Like Milne, Carr, Stevenson and Bates, Roberts had had firsthand experience of the art that Lyman admired most. At nineteen, he had begun his studies at the conservative Ecole des Beaux-arts, in Montreal, and later complained of his teachers' narrow vision; he was shown reproductions of masterpieces, but nothing, Roberts recalled, as recent as Cézanne. (Another student at the school, nearly twenty years later, remembers seeing nothing more recent than Delacroix or Ingres). But in 1927 and 1928, Roberts studied at the Art students League in New York, with John Sloan and Max Weber. He spent much of his time in galleries and museums, studying whatever he could find that compensated for his academic foundation. John Heliker, a fellow student at the League remembers going repeatedly to the Metropolitan Museum with Roberts, to see the Cézannes. Lack of financial backing forced Roberts to return home after two years at the League, but his stay in New York impressed him deeply and nourished him throughout his career. His early experience of challenging and stimulating art seems to have helped him to maintain the quality of his work and his ambition as a painter. It may also have helped him to maintain his independence when he painted landscapes and remain detached from accepted Canadian standards of excellence, as exemplified by the Group of Seven.

Roberts' distinctive style—loosely brushed and solidly constructed—is wholly his own, as is his palette of saturated colors. Bold tonal contrasts clarify color and, at the same time, suggest bulk in Roberts' broadly painted landscapes. (He is also an accomplished painter of figures and still lifes, his winter occupation, when he was unable to work out of doors). Like Milne, Roberts paints a domesticated Canada of farms and woods, not of untamed wilderness. No less intensely felt and no less dramatic than his predecessors' images of unconquered nature, Roberts' hillsides and farmyards are celebrations of habitation, of summer weather and of *enjoyment* of the outdoors. (The only Roberts snow scenes that come to mind are views out a window, of a Montreal street). For all his pleasure in appearance, Roberts is a far from literal painter; instead he invents painterly equivalents for transient nuances of light and atmosphere, translating his acute sensibilities into rich color and vigorous brushwork. It's worth noting, though, that for all the formal liberties Roberts takes with the landscape, his pictures always have a powerful sense of place.

René Richard (1895-1982), a largely self-taught Quebec painter, has almost certainly learned from Roberts' example. Richard's loosely structured, rapidly stroked images of Quebec forests seem to share with Roberts' pictures a simultaneous awareness of the special properties of paint and of location.

Today the condition of landscape painting in Canada is surprisingly healthy. Young, intensely serious artists still feel challenged by the inherent characteristics of their surroundings and still believe that it is possible to make major art about those characteristics. They feel, too, that they are part of a long and potent tradition, peculiar to Canada. Canadians tend to be obsessed by their elusive national identity; they strive to define the qualities that distinguish them from everyone else. The vigor of the Canadian tradition of landscape painting helps to do just that.

Karen Wilkin
New York, 1987

Black Spruce and Maple, 1915, oil on panel, 8⁵⁄₁₆ x 10½″
The Art Gallery of Ontario, Toronto
Gift of Mr. and Mrs. Lawren Harris, 1927

Tom Thomson

1877-1917

A. Y. Jackson
1882-1974

St. Lawrence, North Shore, Winter, c. 1934, oil on board, 8½ x 10½"

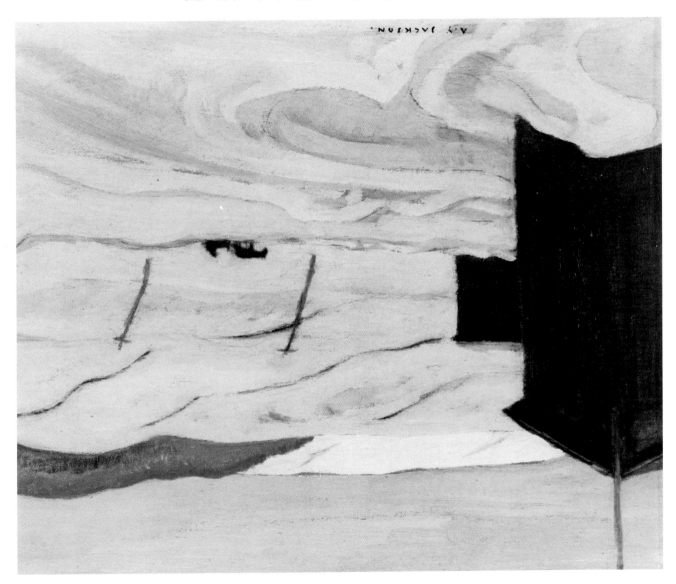

Lake Superior Hill XV, n.d., oil on canvas, 48 x 60¼"

Lawren S. Harris

1885-1970

Dark Pool, c. 1932, oil on canvas, 16 x 20″

David Milne

1882-1953

J.E.H. MacDonald
1873-1932

Larches on Oesa Trail, 1929, oil on board, 8½ x 10½"

Mountains near Kaslo, B.C., c. 1940, pencil on paper, 9 x 11½″

Frederick H. Varley

1881-1969

Alfred J. Casson
1898-

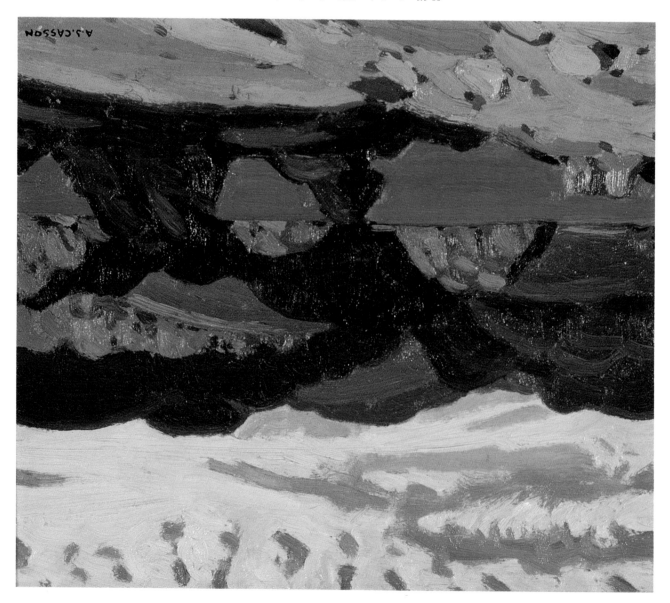

Haliburton Lake, 1923, oil on board, 9¾ x 11¼"

Albert H. Robinson

1881-1956

Fishing Boats, Baie St. Paul, 1929, oil on canvas, 17 x 21"

Edwin H. Holgate
1892-1977

Laurentian Landscape, 1950, oil on panel, 8½ x 10½"

Trappers and Dog Team, 1942, colored pencil on paper, 9½ x 10½″

René Richard
1895-1982

Tree Stump, Vancouver Island, 1953, oil on canvas, 24 x 20″

Arthur Lismer

1885-1969

B. C. Trees, Forest Rhythm, n.d., oil on paper mounted on canvas, 23 x 34¾"

Emily Carr

1871-1945

Charles Comfort
1900-

Mt. Bident Summit, Canadian Rockies, n.d., oil on board, 12 x 16″

Lake in Autumn, 1978, oil on canvas, 24 x 30"

Maxwell Bates

1906-1981

Jack Bush
1909-1977

Grey and Gold, 1943, oil on board, 11 x 8⅝"

Farm Late Afternoon, 1965, oil on board, 32 x 45"

W. Goodridge Roberts
1904-1974

W. L. Stevenson
1905-1966

Trees—Queen Elizabeth Park, Edmonton, n.d., oil on board, 18 x 24"

Spring Sunset—Hockley Valley, 1951, watercolor on paper, 12½ x 17½"

Carl Schaefer

1903-

Catalogue of the Exhibition

Maxwell Bates:

Land of the Haida, 1978, oil on canvas, 20 x 24"
Lake in Autumn, 1978, oil on canvas, 24 x 30"

Jack Bush:

Bass Lake, 1949, oil on board, 11 x 8⅝"
The Bathers, 1946, watercolor, 14¾ x 20¼"
Boats on the Beach, 1946, watercolor, 14½ x 20½"
Drill Day, 1947, oil on board, 11 x 8½"
Grey and Gold, 1943, oil on board, 11 x 8⅝"
House, 1930, watercolor, 9 x 10"
Lake Huron, 1939, oil on board, 8½ x 10¾"
Old House, Hog's Hollow, 1929, oil on board, 8½ x 10¾"
Red, White, and Blue, 1946, watercolor, 14¾ x 21¼"
The Road, 1947, oil on board, 11⅛ x 8½"
Road near Huntsville, 1945, oil, 11 x 8½"
Rocks in Field, 1953, oil on board, 11⅛ x 8⅞"
Small Red Hill, 1953, oil on board, 22⅛ x 17⅛"
The Sumac Tree, c. 1930, watercolor, 9 x 10"
Summer Cottage, 1942, oil on board, 23¼ x 28⅛"
Summer Cottage, 1941, oil on board, 11 x 8¾"
Sunny Day, Winter, 1936, watercolor, 5¾ x 7"

Emily Carr:

B.C. Trees, Forest Rhythm, c. 1934-35, oil on paper/on canvas, 35½ x 23¼"
Her Studio, n.d., oil on canvas, 22¾ x 14½"

A. J. Casson:

Haliburton Lake, 1923, oil on board, 9¼ x 11¼"
Lake of Two Rivers, 1942, oil on panel, 9¾ x 11¼"
Sun After Rain, 1959, oil on canvas, 30 x 38"

Charles Comfort:

Approaching Storm—Algonquin Park, 1946, watercolor, 17 x 22"
Dark Journey, 1946, watercolor, 12¾ x 16¾"
Fallen Leaves, Autumn, 1946, watercolor, 12¾ x 16¾"
Mt. Bident Summit, Canadian Rockies, n.d., oil on board, 12 x 16"
South Point—Starr's Island (Geo. Bay), 1981, oil on board, 12 x 16"

Lawren S. Harris:

Arctic, n.d., pencil on paper, 8 x 10"
Lake Superior Hill XV, oil on canvas, 48 x 60½"
Rocky Mountain—River, n.d., pencil on paper, 8 x 10"
Three Peaks, n.d., pencil on paper, 8 x 10"
View Through the Trees, Algoma, c. 1919, oil on canvas, 10 x 14"
Collection, Mr. Remak Ramsay

Edwin Holgate:

Paysage des Laurentians, 1950, oil on board, 8½ x 10½"

A. Y. Jackson:

Canmore, Alberta, 1945, oil on canvas, 21 x 26"
Gray Day, Gaspé, 1936, oil on board, 8½ x 10⅜"
North Shore, Lake Superior, 1924, oil on board, 8¼ x 10½"
St. Lawrence, North Shore, Winter, c. 1934, oil on board, 8½ x 10½"

Arthur Lismer:

Tree Stump, Vancouver Island, 1953, oil on canvas, 24 x 20"

J. E. H. MacDonald:

Larches on Oesa Trail, 1929, oil on board, 8½ x 10½"

David Milne:

Dark Pool, c. 1932, oil on canvas, 16 x 20"
Driftwood and Sumac, c. 1934, oil on canvas, 12 x 16"
Spreading Shapes, 1915, watercolor, 13 x 18"
Tree and Building Pattern, c. 1915, india ink, 14¾ x 21⅛"
Tree and Fence, 1913, watercolor, 9 x 10"
Twigs in Winter, 1937, oil on canvas, 12 x 14½"

René Richard:

Summer Landscape near Baie St. Paul, c. 1952-53, oil on masonite, 10 x 12"
Trappers Camp Northern Alberta, 1942, colored pencil, 11 x 13½"
Trappers and Dog Team, 1942, colored pencil, 9½ x 10½"

Goodridge Roberts:

Bend in the River, Midsummer, Laurentians, 1953, oil on board, 25 x 32"
Farm Late Afternoon, 1965, oil on board, 32 x 45"
Georgian Bay, 1952, oil on board, 24 x 36"
Hot Summer Sky, 1959, oil on board, 32 x 48"
Late Summer, Laurentians, 1959, oil on board, 25 x 32"
St. Jovite, c. 1938, oil on board, 17 x 21"

A. H. Robinson:

Fishing Boats, Baie St. Paul, 1929, oil on canvas, 17 x 21"
Long Shadows, 1921, oil on panel, 6¾ x 8¼"

Carl Schaefer:

Spring Sunset—Hockley Valley, 1951, watercolor on paper, 12½ x 17½"

W. L. Stevenson:

Autumn Foothills, n.d., oil on board, 12 x 14"

Birches in Queen Elizabeth Park, n.d., oil on board, 16 x 20"

Foothills Lake, n.d., oil on board, 12 x 14"

A Shady Pool, n.d., oil on board, 16 x 20"

Trees—Queen Elizabeth Park, Edmonton, n.d., oil on board, 18 x 24"

West of Calgary, n.d., oil on board, 16 x 20"

Tom Thomson:

Black Spruce and Maple, 1915, oil on panel, 8⁵⁄₁₆ x 10½"
The Art Gallery of Ontario, Toronto
Gift of Mr. and Mrs. Lawren Harris, 1927

Autumn Foliage, n.d., oil on panel, 9 x 11"
Collection of the Edmonton Art Gallery, Edmonton, Alberta
Gift of R. A. Laidlaw, 1954

Selected Bibliography

Terry Fenton and Karen Wilkin. *Modern Painting in Canada* (Edmonton, Alberta: Hurtig Publishers, 1978).

Charles C. Hill. *Canadian Painting in the Thirties* (Ottawa, Ontario: The National Gallery of Canada, 1975).

Roald Nasgaard. *The Mystic North* (Toronto, Ontario: Art Gallery of Ontario, 1984).

John O'Brian. *David Milne and the Modern Tradition of Painting* (Toronto, Ontario: Coach House Press, 1983).

Dennis Reid. *A Concise History of Canadian Painting* (Toronto, Ontario: Oxford University Press, 1973).

Dennis Reid. *The Group of Seven/Le Groupe des Sept* (Ottawa, Ontario: The National Gallery of Canada, 1970).

Doris Shadbolt. *The Art of Emily Carr* (Seattle, Washington: University of Washington Press, 1979).

Christopher Varley. *The Contemporary Art Society* (Edmonton, Alberta: The Edmonton Art Gallery, 1980).

Karen Wilkin, ed. *Jack Bush* (Toronto, Ontario: McLelland and Stewart, 1984).

David Wistow. *Tom Thomson and the Group of Seven* (Toronto, Ontario: Art Gallery of Ontario, 1982).

The Grace Borgenicht Gallery offers our sincere thanks
to the International Cultural Relations Bureau of the
Department of External Affairs, Canada and the
Canadian Consulate General, New York for their
support and assistance.

The Grace Borgenicht Gallery extends our gratitude to
Karen Wilkin for her work in organizing this exhibition
as well as for her introductory essay.

Editorial production: Caroline Adler

Photography: Thomas Moore Photography,
            Wm. Notman & Son,
            Sarah Wells

Graphic design: Julie Graham

Printing: Canfield Printing

GRACE BORGENICHT GALLERY